The Door Is Not Locked

Finding Happiness

in the

Real World

Roger Cornwall

Copyright © 2015 by Roger Cornwall
All rights reserved. This book or any portion thereof may not be reproduced or used in any manner whatsoever without the express written permission of the publisher except for the use of brief quotations in a book review.

Printed in the United States of America
First Printing, 2015

ISBN-13: 978-1522904632
ISBN-10: 1522904638

Contents

PREFACE		i
THE JOURNEY BEGINS		1
1.	The Door Is Not Locked	3
2.	What Else Is Possible?	9
NAVIGATING THE MIND		15
3.	Say "Ah" and Open Up	17
4.	Do Not Want What You Would Like	23
5.	You Cannot Be Sad	29
NAVIGATING THE WORLD		39
6.	Love Losing or Lose Loving	41
7.	Let Yourself Succeed	48
8.	I Am Not the Messiah!	55
REACHING ENLIGHTENMENT		65
9.	The Experiment Always Works	67
10.	The Freedom of Captivity	76
11.	Sitting at the Loom of Life	84
THANK YOU		91

Preface

I am distinctly unqualified to write this book. I am not a psychologist. I am not a Buddhist monk. I am not a spiritual leader. I am not a motivational speaker. I am just a man who struggles with his own life and all of its challenges. I have been blessed with miracles, yet I have been to the depths of depression. I have felt fortunate to be alive, yet saddled by life's burdens. I am just like you. So as I write this book, it is from the perspective of a person, not a professional. If you read these pages, maybe a few of them, maybe all of them, and feel that you can relate, then maybe I have accomplished the goal of making you realize you are not alone. You are not the only one who falls into mental and emotional traps without an obvious way out. Even better, if you learn some ideas that can guide you out of those traps and help you on your own path to true happiness, then perhaps this book has served a higher purpose.

Whatever you get out of it, just know that I wrote it initially for myself. To organize my thoughts on my own path to happiness. To practice the learnings I have picked up along the way. So when you read these pages, you will be joining me on this path, not in a linear story of my journey, but in an exploration of the pearls of wisdom I have learned to use and the pitfalls I have learned to avoid.

It is a short book, organized by themes, and it can be read cover to cover or in a piecemeal fashion. You can read any number of chapters and in any order, for each chapter tells a story in its own right. Moreover, the chapters contain only some of the many "Aha" moments I have encountered – I am still always learning. And I still need to practice what I know. You will be practicing along with me. We are all on our own journeys, following different paths, but we all seek the same goal, even if we don't know it:

Happiness.

So whether you are looking for empathy or guidance on your journey to happiness, you will find exactly what you need, for only you know what you need. But try to keep an open mind, for you will only understand what you are ready to understand. It is all there already, inside your mind, inside the door to happiness. And that door is not locked. You just need to walk through it. Join me and we will walk through it together.

THE JOURNEY BEGINS

-1-

THE DOOR IS NOT LOCKED

In the eighth grade, a friend and I did a spontaneous experiment. I don't know why – perhaps as a prank – but it has turned out to be quite instructive. We arrived at our homeroom class a little early, but didn't go in. We decided to stand outside the door to see if anyone else would stand outside the door with us. We knew the teacher was in the room, as we had seen her walking around, but she then went to her desk, which was not within view from the door. When the next student arrived, we told him that the door was locked. The teacher must be late. When the next student arrived, we did the same thing. After that, we didn't have to say anything. The entire class arrived one by one, each one standing outside the door with us, with conversations starting about how strange it was that the teacher was late. "Do we get to go home?" "What about our homework?" The funny part was that no one tried the door. They all believed it was locked. Or they were too afraid to try the handle and fail to open it, provoking jeers from their peers when they failed.

Decades later, I realized I was one of those kids standing outside the door. But it was a different door. It wasn't the door to an eighth grade classroom. It was the door to happiness.

The pursuit of happiness is supposedly an unalienable right, so by God, we will pursue it! We are bombarded by advice on how to pursue happiness. Get that job, get that promotion, buy a nice car, marry a hot spouse, win that game or race, become famous, etc. Then you'll be happy. And when those goals fail and we find ourselves unhappy, we are told to drink. "Man, I need a beer!" Even when those goals succeed, and we are still unhappy, we are told we need to drink to relax from our stress of trying to achieve those goals. "Happy hour" is indeed quite a telling name for what our society sees as the antidote to the stress of pursuing happiness. As if we shouldn't be happy when we work, we shouldn't be happy when we get home, but for one hour, if we drink enough discounted alcohol, we have permission to be happy.

In fact, it is almost unavoidable to learn from our society that alcohol is the key to the door of happiness.

But the door is not locked!

We are all eighth graders standing outside an unlocked door, unable to get through the door because our peers' beliefs and behaviors are inadvertently telling us we can't. But we don't need permission to open the door to happiness. We don't need a key. We don't need to achieve financial, professional, performance, or social goals to get through the door. It is not only unlocked; it is automatic. It will open for us. So why is it so hard to get through that damned door?

I, and I'm sure you can relate, have been pushing hard on that door for many years. Maybe I just needed to push harder. Maybe I needed someone to push with me. Maybe I needed someone to push *for* me. Despair set in: maybe it doesn't really open. Then one day I realized that I was that guy in the Far Side cartoon pushing hard on the door to the Midvale School for the Gifted that was clearly marked "PULL". I was pushing on a door that opened towards me.

So naturally, once I got over the embarrassment (surely someone saw me pushing on that door), I started pulling like mad. But with all my strength I couldn't open that door. It wouldn't budge. Maybe all the baggage I had accumulated in my pursuit of happiness was still surrounding me and blocking the door. So I set out to get rid of that baggage. I got a therapist. Two, actually. I got a life coach. I laid myself bare at home and at work. I aggressively shed all of the unnecessary crap that I was carrying around with me. And when I felt free of as much baggage as I could shed, I walked right up to that door again. I grasped the handle. I pulled. And nothing happened. Shit! What was I missing?

Have you ever walked up to an automatic swinging door and wondered why it didn't open? You assume since it says "automatic" that there must be a sensor somewhere, so you start waving your arms around. You see a blinking red light on an electronic device over the door. Does that mean it's working? Or does that mean it's broken? You stand there feeling increasingly uneasy until someone walks up and says "you're standing too close to the door." You take one step back and the door opens toward you. The door had been programmed to not whack you in the face while you were standing in its way. Yet you curse the door because it was impeding your forward progress. It slowed you down; it made you stop, and even take a step backwards. Who would design such a contraption?

That, my friend, is the door to happiness.

You cannot force open the door to happiness. You cannot push it or pull it. You cannot charge forth in your breakneck pursuit of happiness and expect the door to simply get out of your way. You must stop, take a step back, and let it open. It doesn't matter how many of your friends and family members are pushing and pulling on their doors, or expecting someone else to open their doors for them. It doesn't matter how many people are sitting slumped up against their doors to happiness, drinking away their need to go through the door. Take a step back and your door will open automatically.

The trouble is that we have been taught in our culture that taking a step backwards is a bad thing. That it is a failure. So we have gotten very good at putting one foot in front of the other, no matter what. And we are terrible at willfully taking a step back. We don't want to do it. We let ourselves believe we shouldn't do it. We even let ourselves believe we can't do it. But centuries of wisdom have independently concluded that taking a step back is the only path to true happiness. Call it enlightenment, higher consciousness, spirituality, Zen, "the zone", or whatever you want. There is a space of awareness in our mind from which we can watch the world flow by and feel truly happy. When we take a step back into that space in our mind, the door to happiness opens before us.

For me, it was hitting the rock bottom of depression and being forced to choose "up" as a direction since there was no further down I could go. Upon realizing that I had the power to separate myself from my downward emotional spiral, I started exploring that power – reading, meditating, learning. And then it hit me. I had been no better than those eighth grade classmates of mine, duped by my peers to stand blindly outside a door to happiness that I thought was locked. The only thing separating me from those eighth-graders was a few decades of searching for a key for that unlocked door. I just had to get out of its way, let it open, and then walk through it.

And so I did. And here's what I saw.

-2-

What Else Is Possible?

You've probably shopped for a car before. First, you decide what sort of car you need – sedan, SUV, convertible, minivan, etc – what will meet your needs. Then you start your research. You set a budget. You look at all the facts and reviews and compare prices. You look at pictures, you test drive a few, you make a preliminary decision. You even decide on a color. Maybe bright orange – that'll be unique, just like you. And then, suddenly, you see that exact car all over the place. It seems as though every intersection has one of those cars. In fact, it seems to be one of the most common cars on the road. Especially bright orange ones! Are they suddenly the most popular car? Did everyone simultaneously decide it was the car to own? Maybe it's a great car after all. Or maybe it's too popular for you now. But where were all these cars before? Why didn't you see them everywhere until today?

Those cars were there the whole time. Even the bright orange ones. You just didn't notice them because they weren't on the front of your mind. They might not have been on your mind at all, before you knew anything about them, or before you decided to shop for a car. The images came into your eyes and rifled through the part of your mind that processes images, but never made it to the part of your mind that assigns importance or meaning to them. Only once you had meaning associated with those images did you notice them consciously.

But so what? What do bright orange cars have to do with happiness?

Here's the trouble with not noticing bright orange cars. You only pay attention to the conscious part of your mind most of the time. You hear nagging from other parts, but you let your conscious mind call the shots. And your conscious mind is fueled by what you let into it – what you notice. And you tend to only notice that which already has meaning in your conscious mind. Do you see a vicious cycle here? We all wear lenses, built by our past, through which we see the present. The effect is that our view gets narrower and narrower by noticing only that which reinforces what we are already thinking. That process creates a rut. That rut in which our thinking gets stuck becomes narrower and deeper over time. And boy is it ever easy to get stuck in that rut.

We can know when we are stuck in a rut. Boredom slowly grows into despair, and then into anger. We then defensively lash out at a world that is obviously there to hurt us. We truly believe that the hurt we feel is coming directly at us from a world that is only out to hurt us. Why? Because that is the way we see the world when we feel hurt. It's the vicious cycle.

Like you perhaps, there have been times that those feelings have overwhelmed me. In those moments, a trusted advisor has often told me to ask myself, "What else is possible?" I never fully realized the power of that question until after I had stumbled through the door of happiness. For only then did I begin to see that something else might *actually* be possible. Once I walked through that door, I started to see my life, past and present, in a different way. I started to see examples of many of the principles of enlightenment in the real world. They had been there all along – the bright orange cars – I just wasn't noticing them.

I only had to look outside my rut. I only had to become aware of the power of awareness. Awareness not connected to preconceived notions, or meanings, or values. Just plain and simple awareness. Seeing the bright orange cars without shopping for one. Letting things in that you haven't let in before. Just to see what's out there. You will be amazed at how much meaning can appear, at how much is possible. The eighth grade classroom door is just one such example. The coming chapters contain other examples of some of the principles that have appeared along my path to happiness. I didn't find them – they found me – I just let myself notice them.

We each live individual lives with unique perspectives on the world around us, so treat the examples in this book as uniquely of my own perspective. But I hope that they resonate with you on some level. I hope you are able to glean from them a sense that what *you* experience may not be what you think at first, that there may be another way of looking at something. We are so steadfast in our beliefs and perceptions, so stuck in our ruts of thinking and seeing, that it is very difficult to entertain alternative explanations of life and alternative solutions to our problems. However, if for one fleeting second we believe that something else could be possible, we open the door to a whole new world. So as you read these stories, reflect on what they might mean in your life by asking yourself the question:

What else is possible?

Navigating the Mind

-3-

Say "Ah" and Open Up

Have you ever washed a 4-year-old boy's hair? How about twin 4-year-old boys at the same time? Once you have corralled them into the bathroom and convinced them that they want to get into the bathtub, you have to get them wet. And not just the part of them that they want to get wet, but their hair too. And not just once, but twice – once to get the hair ready for the shampoo, and once to get the shampoo out. If you're particularly unlucky, you have children with thick hair that is practically unbrushable unless you use conditioner, which means you have to get their hair wet yet again to rinse it out. Three times! Three times you have to convince these cats to get their hair wet. What's more, you have to get their hair wet without getting their eyes wet, or full of shampoo or conditioner, and all while they're moving; nay, convulsing. You know that if they would just tilt their heads back and hold still it would be easy. But that's not how it happens, and it is anything but easy.

All you can think about is how lovely it would be to be standing in a shower yourself with your head tilted back, letting hot water run over your hair. Few moments are as blissful as that. Especially after a long day, when you're cranky and exhausted. Or after a long camping trip, when you're extra dirty, or after a long workout, when you're extra sweaty. It seems that no matter what happens in the day, you can rinse it all away by letting warm water flow over your head. So why is it so awful for 4-year-old boys, especially when they're cranky, exhausted, dirty, and sweaty? How is it that a moment can be for you a pleasurable escape but for your children a form of torture? You're thinking about an outdoor shower at a spa in Costa Rica; they're thinking about boiling oil being poured on them from the ramparts.

How can we teach these kids to enjoy rinsing their hair as much as we do? There is nothing inherently painful about it; how can we teach them to be OK with it instead of hating it?

Which raises a bigger question: how can we teach *ourselves* to tolerate or even enjoy those moment in our life that we tend to resist?

In stumbling across a way to peacefully rinse my children's hair, I learned an answer to this question. Believe me: the answer arrived by dumb luck. I tried everything. I tried gently scooping up water in my hands; I tried using a cup, a plastic toy boat, a handheld shower nozzle. I tried reasoning with them. I tried begging, threatening punishment, letting them do it themselves. I tried sneaking up on them with a bucket of water from behind and then apologizing. But no matter what, it was a brutal experience for all of us. "You got soap in my eyes!" "Of course I did – you wouldn't hold still!" "But how can I hold still when you're getting soap in my eyes?" Until one day, in a moment of what turned out to be accidental brilliance, I told one son to tilt his head back and say "Ah" as the water ran through his hair. Not the "Open up and say Ah" kind of "Ah" that you say when the doctor has a tongue suppressor pushed halfway down your sore throat. But the sort of "Ah" that you say when your butt hits the couch after all the children are in bed, hair washed and rinsed, and you are finally able to rest and relax. To my great surprise, when my son tilted his head back and said "Ah" as I poured the water over his head, he smiled! He smiled as if he actually *enjoyed* the process. He held still, his hair got rinsed, and no shampoo got in his eyes. Then his twin brother said "do that to me!" clearly eager to experience that kind of enjoyment. I told him the same thing. Say "Ah". He did, and he enjoyed it too. From that moment on, rinsing hair has not been a problem.

Why on earth did that work?

We can assign whatever emotion we want to any moment in our life. However, we have a tendency to let the moment assign the emotion. We relinquish what is perhaps our greatest power, delegating the determination of our emotional state to the world around us. It was not my children's idea to get their hair wet, so they resisted it. But in the process, they let the resistance assign a negative emotion to the experience. By saying "Ah", as if they enjoyed it, they actually enjoyed it! They learned on the first try that they have the power to assign a positive emotion to the experience. They simply made a commitment to enjoy it, symbolized that commitment by saying "Ah," and it worked. We all have the power to make that same commitment, that same choice. But we must use it.

It is not easy. How many times have you heard someone tell you to "look on the bright side"? And how many times have you wanted to punch them in the face? How annoying was Bobby McFerrin's song "Don't Worry, Be Happy"? Easy for a Grammy-winning celebrity to say. And how ridiculous was Monty Python's "Always look on the bright side of life" sung by Eric Idle nailed to a cross? When we are in a bad place, the last thing we want to hear is someone telling us we should be in a good place. How are we supposed to look on the bright side of a world that is hurting us at the moment? But that's the very problem – even if we look on the bright side of life, we are still letting the world assign our emotions (if we could just find the bright side of the world, then the world would be able to give us the positive emotions we need).

But emotions are not the world's to give.

We, and only we, feel our own emotions. We are conditioned to feel certain ways about certain experiences. But we don't have to believe what we are taught. What we really believe is what we feel. Just ask my kids: did they really believe they were happy getting their hair rinsed when they said "Ah"? Yes, they did. Why? Because they made it so. They weren't happy *because* they were getting their hair rinsed – they were simply happy *while* they were getting their hair rinsed. Their happiness had nothing to do with the rinsing of their hair. It was simply a result of choosing happiness. We can do the same thing. We can choose whatever emotion we want – even happiness. Whenever we want – even when something is bothering us. We just have to believe that we can.

I have practiced what my children taught me. Sometimes when I have a minute or two to myself, instead of thinking about all that is worrying me, or trying not to think about all that is worrying me, I have tried simply saying "Ah", as if it is the happiest moment of my day. Like nothing could be better. And I have realized a profound and consistent effect. Genuinely (not sarcastically or bitterly) expressing happiness actually opens my mind to feeling happiness. So choose happiness and express it, and doing so will open your mind to the ability to feel it.

So say "Ah" and open up.

-4-

Do Not Want What You Would Like

My father grew up in New Zealand during the Great Depression. Yes, he's been around for a while - he turns 90 this Christmas Eve. He has seen quite a bit during those 90 years. He left high school to fight in World War II. After the war, he traveled the world, working as an airplane mechanic in half a dozen countries before settling down to go to college upon the advice of a boss who essentially fired him for being too smart to build aircraft engines. He is now a professor emeritus of a university history department that he led for 17 years. His rich life has nurtured in him a unique combination of intellect, worldliness, and satisfaction with minimal needs. So I have always appreciated his perspective on any aspect of life. However, despite a gift for teaching hundred-student classes with wit and wisdom, he rarely shared his personal thoughts at home.

All that changed when he had a debilitating stroke twelve years ago. Robbed of basic physical functions but fully intellectually intact, he found a new value in communication as a form of participation in life. Since regaining his speech, he hasn't stop talking. Stories, commentary, ideas, complaints, questions, laughter, tears, wisdom – the wealth of his mind has come pouring out. But it hasn't all been pleasant. As a self-sufficient, fighting-spirit sort of person, he struggled mightily with his new dependence on others for help, and that struggle was clear. But that struggle has evolved into acceptance, and even celebration, of his new life. And through that journey, he has risen to stardom in my mind. No, he will never be on the news for running a marathon at 90. He will never be revered by our society for being youthful despite his age. Because that's what our society does: we are taught to respect only those elderly folks who defy their age, not those folks who celebrate their age. My father lived in Japan, where the elderly are respected for what they uniquely possess – age - for with age comes experience, and with experience, wisdom. Not so in America. He has always lamented that fact about our society.

He has also lamented our bizarre use of the English language. He grew up in a former British colony speaking the Queen's English, and never really understood why we butchered the language so badly in America. I used to think he was just complaining about American culture in an elitist sort of way, but the importance of language became clear to me the last time I visited him a few weeks ago. I asked him what he wanted for his upcoming ninetieth birthday, and he replied:

"While there are things I would like, there is nothing I want."

Huh? What on earth did he mean by that? What's the difference? In the answer to that question lies a clue to satisfaction, gratitude, and happiness.

American English is indeed strange. There are often multiple meanings to words. Some words start off with one meaning and evolve into meaning something totally different. Sometimes, a word may be a noun in one context and a verb in another. Words may even transition from noun to verb and vice versa. Take the word "gift" for example. "Gift" used to be something you give. Then, as more and more people admitted to not liking gifts they had been given, they started passing those gifts on to other people instead of keeping them for themselves. The process of "re-gifting" was born. And if you can "re-gift" something, surely you can "gift" it. Suddenly "gift" became a verb in addition to being a noun. I was quite alarmed when a prodigious engineer from Stanford University, from whom I was purchasing a piece of groundbreaking research technology, suggested that he would "gift" me some components of the technology during a trial period. Here's someone with an advanced degree, who is so intelligent that he left his faculty position to start a company based on the novelty of his invention, using a noun as a verb. It's official. "Gift" is now both a noun and a verb.

Once a word becomes both a noun and a verb, it has two meanings, or at least two connotations. And those connotations can trick us. Now consider the word I used in my question to my father: "want". We commonly use this word as a verb, meaning to desire, crave, etc. But it is also a noun, meaning "a lack or deficiency of something", according to the Oxford

English Dictionary. Although most dictionaries describe the noun form of "want" to be archaic, it still hangs on in our language today as a connotation at the very least. So when we say we want something, we are implying that we lack it or are deficient in it. We are tricked into focusing, even subconsciously, on the lack or absence of something in our lives.

You probably want something right now. Perhaps you want more money. You want more success. You want a better marriage, career, life. Whatever it is that you want, what if I told you that you would never get it? Let's take money for example. What if I told you that you would never make more money? If that is something that you want, how would you react? Who and how would you be without that want being satisfied? You would think of a *lack* of more money. You would be unable to celebrate your existing riches because of the unfulfilled "want." You would be unsatisfied, incomplete, diminished. There is grave danger in wanting, in the traditional sense of the word: we all-too-often rely on the satisfaction of our wants to determine our happiness, where unfulfilled wants intrinsically mean unfulfilled happiness.

So stop "wanting". And start "would liking."

What's the difference, you ask? The difference lies in the word, "would", which implies an "if". *If I were to have more money, I would like it.* And anywhere there is an "if", there is a possibility rather than certainty. *It's not certain that I'll ever have more money.* And anywhere there is merely a possibility of something rather than certainty of it, we do not allow ourselves to expect it. *I cannot expect to have more money.* And if we refrain from expecting something, we open the door to being comfortable with the idea of not getting it. *For now I have to live with the money I have.* And once we allow ourselves to become comfortable with the notion that we may only ever have that which we already have, we can learn to appreciate and even celebrate it. No matter how little or how much it is. We can become truly grateful, no matter what. And with true gratefulness comes true happiness.

That is why my father is so happy. He has a cabin that keeps him warm through the cold Alaskan winters. He has a loving and tirelessly devoted wife, a comfortable chair, some good books, and a sleep schedule that allows him to watch football (what Americans call "soccer" for some strange reason) while it's being played live in England. And there is nothing that he wants.

Although he has said that he *would* like it if I called home more often.

-5-

You Cannot Be Sad

I had the great fortune of studying in Paris toward the end of my surgical training, so my wife and I were able to live there for a month. While you might think that a month in Paris would be dreamy, it did not start off well. We had spent the preceding month in South Africa, basking in the warmth, beauty and hospitality of Cape Town. It was January while we were in South Africa, so it was the middle of the summer. So when we went to Paris in February, it was suddenly the middle of winter. That was a shock, but not nearly the shock we experienced in the change of culture. Especially the attitude toward Americans. Especially Americans who try to speak French!

We arrived close to the middle of the night, dropped our two months' worth of luggage in our small rental apartment, and set out to find an open restaurant for some much needed dinner. We had chosen to stay in a residential part of Paris in order to get a flavor of real Paris. Which meant we were far from any tourist-friendly restaurants. Parisians fortunately like to dine late though, so we were able to find one place open. It looked warm inside, and we were starving, so we went in.

We were handed menus, written only in French of course, but I didn't think that would be a problem. I took four years of French in high school. I studied French philosophy texts, performed French plays, and wrote French poetry. So I thought I could take a stab at a French menu. Little did I realize, however, how badly 15 years of intervening time without speaking or reading French had rusted my skills. Nonetheless, I was able to find a dish I knew I liked: andouillette. I love andouille sausage in gumbo and jambalaya, French-Cajun dishes. So a plate of hot andouille sausage sounded great on this cold night.

The waiter arrived, took my wife's order, and then turned to me. I summoned my best French, "Andouillette, si vous plait", or "andouillette, please." Yes, I had forgotten how to say the first part: "I would like the..." The waiter looked me up and down with a quizzical, semi-concerned look on his face. He said something in French that I think meant, "are you sure", but that was more from the look on his face than any understanding of his Parisian French. Confident in my ability to handle spicy food (andouille sausage can be spicy), I answered "oui", or "yes". With a chuckle, the waiter turned and returned to the kitchen. I thought it was rude that he would laugh, but I knew that Parisians can behave coldly to foreigners who try to speak their language.

But that was not why he had laughed. As soon as the dish arrived, I knew why.

Andouillette is not andouille sausage. Andouillette is intestines. Tripe. Wrapped up in a casing and cooked, then cut out for your gustatory pleasure. Now I knew why he was laughing. He knew I had no idea what it was, and he let me fall for my own ignorance, my hubristically dangerous semi-understanding of French.

I don't like eating intestines. Not in the least bit. No matter how hungry I am. Needless to say I didn't eat it. When the waiter returned at the end of our meal, my plate was still full. He asked me something else I didn't understand, motioning toward my plate, so I assumed he was asking if I was done. I replied, "Je suis fini", or "I am finished". He laughed again. But this time he corrected me: "J'ai fini". My high school French lessons came rushing back into my mind. I remember mistakenly saying "je suis fini" before, and being told that in French, that means I am done-for, dead, gone from this earth. The proper saying is "j'ai fini", or "I *have* finished," meaning I have finished my meal, my project, my whatever. But the waiter didn't have to laugh! It was like rubbing salt in a wound.

On that cold night in Paris, I was humiliated, nauseated, and still starving, so I saw no humor or wisdom in the grammatical correction of my obviously terrible French. However, now, many years later, the seemingly unimportant difference between "je suis fini" and "j'ai fini" carries critical meaning on the journey to happiness.

Who *are* you? I mean, what defines you? Your name? Your occupation? Your position in your family? That's a hard question to answer, because no matter what answer you provide, there is a time in your life that you weren't that thing, that descriptor. I am a surgeon, but I wasn't when I was in medical school. Does that mean I changed who I am? Or does that mean who I am is something that transcends titles like surgeon or medical student? What about your name? My wife was not given a name until several days after she was born. Does that mean she wasn't anything for several days? No, your name is not who you are. So what is it that defines *you*? It's actually impossible to answer – we simply don't have the perspective or language to describe the essence of our being.

But that doesn't stop us from trying. We are constantly trying to portray who we are. We consciously paint a picture of our identity to others by choosing what clothes we wear, what persona or avatar we post online, what career we choose.

After my freshman year in a Catholic high school, my brother and I switched to a large public school. I knew no friends at that new school, so I had to make a good first impression. I had to choose which clique of students I would join, because I couldn't handle being a loner (someone who doesn't fit in at least somewhere). And I knew that I would be labeled based on my clothes within minutes of walking into that school. So what did I wear? My Judas Priest t-shirt with the black ¾ length sleeves of course! I liked heavy metal, and I was proud of it, so that's the persona I brought to school that day. Sure enough, I was absorbed instantly into the group of like-minded folks and became known as a "stoner". Leather jackets, torn jeans, chains, studded bracelets, the whole nine yards. I didn't participate in any of the illicit activities that earned that group its name, since I also studied hard and competed at a national level in gymnastics, so I didn't want to jeopardize those pursuits. But I never made it with the nerds or jocks. Because I wore that Judas Priest t-shirt to school, I was a stoner.

That identity stuck with me all the way through graduation three years later. At graduation, as I arose to deliver my commencement address as the valedictorian, a student leaned to the person sitting next to him (who happened to be a friend of mine who told me about it later), and whispered, "I thought we voted that the valedictorian would speak at graduation?" My friend replied, "He is the valedictorian." Shocked, the other student replied, "But he's a stoner!" I truly had become that t-shirt!

I don't wear Judas Priest t-shirts today, but I still like heavy metal. Am I different person? No. Clearly it's not our external appearance that defines us, no matter how we use external features to identify and categorize ourselves and others. But that is not the most dangerous part. The most dangerous part is how we portray who we are to *ourselves*. Internally. Sometimes consciously and sometimes unconsciously. Sometimes in a positive light and sometimes in a negative light. When we feel good, we tell ourselves how proud we are of ourselves. When we feel bad, we call ourselves names, we berate ourselves. Sometimes we say those things out loud, half hoping to hear the reassuring chorus of "don't be so hard on yourself" from our friends and loved ones. Hoping for someone to disagree and to make us feel better. But we don't always know when we are being hard on ourselves, and that's the problem. If we don't recognize it, we can't stop it. If we don't recognize it, we can't verbalize it to seek reassurance. It, the negative self-view, can take over without us even knowing. We can fall into a trap and not even know we've been trapped.

Our language can be just that kind of trap.

Let's go back to Paris. "Je suis fini" literally means "I am finished". That which is me, my very existence, is finished. Which is why the waiter laughed when I said it. Conversely, "J'ai fini" means "I have finished", which implies that there is an object – a meal, a book, a job – that has been finished. Something separate from yourself. It's pretty easy to consider your dinner as something separate from yourself – no one's going to confuse you with a pile of andouillette – so this may seem like a silly argument over semantics. But now let's consider how we describe our emotions:

"I am sad."

By saying that statement in that way, we are defining ourselves by the emotion. We convince ourselves subconsciously that we *are* the emotion. We make it harder for ourselves to see the emotion as something separate from ourselves, like our dinner. Even if we know on some cerebral level that the emotion may not last forever, we allow ourselves to become fully identified by the emotion for that moment, consumed by the emotion, nothing without the emotion. We *become* the emotion. That view makes it nearly impossible to let the emotion pass. We are instantly sucked into the emotion's rut, and from there, we have an uphill battle to climb out. We usually slide further down instead, as if in quicksand.

Now consider alternative ways to express that same emotion:

"I feel sad."

Or even better yet: "I feel sadness."

Said in that way, we begin to see that the emotions are something separate from our identity. This subtle but important shift in language opens the door to two extremely helpful concepts: (1) that we have an identity – a sense of self – that is not defined by our current emotions, no matter how strong, and (2) that the emotion can be allowed to pass without giving up part or all of our identity. The more you become invested in an emotion, the more you identify with it, the harder it is to let it go. We hold on dearly to even the most painful emotions because we allow ourselves to become defined by them.

But an emotion is merely something we feel, something we witness, something that we can watch enter – and then exit – our minds. We just need to sit and watch it without getting married to it. We need to avoid thinking that we *are* the emotion. Just like we can never *be* an occupation, a name, a t-shirt, a plate of andouillette, we can never *be* an emotion. So next time you feel sadness, don't allow yourself to say you are sad, because you can never *be* sad. Feel the sadness, acknowledge it, experience it, witness it, but don't let our strange language trick you into thinking that you have *become* it. Once you recognize the sadness as something separate from yourself, you'll be surprised how easily it can be let go, and how quickly it can go.

NAVIGATING THE WORLD

-6-

Love Losing or Lose Loving

It was 2:00 PM. I looked up as far as I could to try to see the summit, but all I could see was white all around me. A cloud had crept up the mountain I was climbing, creating a total whiteout. I looked down at my footprints disappearing down the slope. I could only see about ten feet down, even though I had been climbing for hours. I looked at the snow in front of me - and by in front of me, I mean 12 inches from my face. The slope was steep, and the snow was waist-deep from a week of steady snow fall. I didn't know how much further up the summit was – I hadn't seen it in an hour because of the whiteout. But I knew it was close. I had mentally marked rock outcroppings before embarking on the final pitch, and I think I was only about 100 feet from the top based on the rock immediately to my right. But it would be slow going to get to the summit. The snow was too deep for crampons to help much, and the slope was too steep for snowshoes. But I knew I could make it. I had plenty of water, plenty of food, plenty of energy. And finding the direction was easy, even in a whiteout: I just had to go up.

But it was 2PM. I had told myself when I set off at 7AM that I would turn around at 2PM, no matter how far I had climbed, so that I could return safely in daylight.

I had a decision to make: go up or go down.

I am an analytical person – perhaps maybe too much so, or so say people who know me well (read: wife and therapist). So naturally I analyzed the situation. I mentally made a table of pros and cons for pushing for the summit. First, the pros. If I went up, I would be able to say I made it to the summit. I would have the satisfaction of conquering the mountain. Would I be able to prove it? No. I had forgotten to bring my GPS watch (I was left to navigate by map and compass – old school), and I was alone on the climb. Would I be able to enjoy the view from the top, perhaps take a picture, a summit selfie? No. It was a whiteout, remember. But I would have bragging rights – the first claim to an ascent (and solo at that!) of this particular mountain in the

Alaska Range. That would be cool. That would help my self-esteem, right?

But at what cost? There were clear cons of going up. The primary concern was running out of daylight on the way back. I had a light, but not enough to navigate in the dark, especially during a whiteout. I didn't have the gear with me for an overnight on the mountain, so I had to get back. I could also run out of food at some point. In addition, the climb had become increasingly treacherous, and it wasn't looking any easier on the topo map toward the summit. That meant an increasingly slow pace and an escalating risk of injury, say for example, from an avalanche. There was a real and palpable risk of death.

So at this point in the analysis, I was essentially trying to decide if it was worth it to risk death to summit this peak. There was joy at the summit, mine for the taking, but there was risk along the way. Would I accept that risk and go for the joy, or would I concede defeat and retreat with my tail between my legs? That would mean failure. I had told everyone at home that I was going to try for the summit. I was going to climb that mountain. How would I tell them that I had failed? What excuses could I come up with? What would they think of me? Or wait...maybe I could just tell them that I did reach the summit. There would be no way to prove or disprove it. Remember, no GPS watch tracking me. And I was pretty darned close. No, that would be lying, and that wouldn't bring me the joy of actually summiting. What was I going to do?

This discussion in my head went on for what felt like hours. I had carved a seat in the snow and was looking out at the slope beside me as I was weighing the pros and cons of ascending further. And then as if to signal the approaching clarity in my mind, the clouds started to clear around me. I began to see the slope of the mountain. I began to see the neighboring peaks. I began to see the glacier below me. And my decision was suddenly clear. I knew exactly what I had to do.

Go back down.

What? I was so close to the top and the conditions were improving! Why the hell would I go down?

Have you ever loved someone? I mean really loved someone? Let's say you love your wife dearly. She enters a marathon, trains for months, and discovers that if she runs hard on race day she could qualify for Boston. Race day comes, and she misses the qualifying time by 2 minutes. Do you still love her? Of course you do! Now let's say it's because it was much hotter than expected on race day, and she had to slow down at mile 20 to avoid heat stroke. Do you still love her? Of course you do! Even more maybe, as you admire her smart decision and think about the pain of potentially seeing her hurt. In fact, the more you love her, the less you care about her marathon finishing time.

So why should it be any different for yourself? Why should you love yourself based on your finishing times? Why should your love for yourself take such a huge hit when you fall short of a goal? Like not reaching the summit.

We spend an entire lifetime trying to love ourselves. Yet we spend most of that lifetime faking it. Our society rewards externally validated success – mountains climbed, marathons run, money earned – and so do we. We put oval "26.2" bumper stickers on our cars to show what we've done, what we can do, in order to validate our worth. We put those same stickers in our mind, measuring our self-worth by what we have done, what we can do. And when we fail to earn another sticker, our self-worth takes a hit. Why? Because all those oval stickers have obscured the path to true self-worth. Sometimes we have to lose a sticker or two to find our way.

Sitting in the snow on a remote mountainside, surrounded by the vast and timeless beauty of the Alaska Range, I lost a sticker. In so doing, I lost a battle that I shouldn't have been fighting. Not with the mountain, but with myself. I didn't really set out to conquer the mountain (it's been there for millions of years and doesn't give a damn if I climb it or not). I realized that I had actually set out to patch a hole in my self-worth by winning another sticker. Only by losing that sticker did I actually realize that I didn't need it. Only by losing did I learn. And what I learned was love. At that moment, I felt an overwhelming sense of love. For the mountain, for the moment, for life, and yes, for myself. Not in the cocky, I'm-a-bad-ass-on-a-mountain kind of way – but in a genuine, unconditional, calm, real way – unlike anything I had ever experienced. I had never felt physically smaller, relative to the monstrous landscape that had thwarted my plans, yet I had never felt spiritually larger and more fulfilled. And for that joy, much greater than the joy of reaching the summit (which I've experienced before), I learned to love losing.

Losing is a far better teacher than winning. We need to learn to love losing for what it can teach us. The trouble is that we only teach ourselves and our children to love winning. Forget Vince Lombardi – the "winning is everything" starts way before pro football. Insanely aggressive youth sports, trash-talking Nike shirts for toddlers, even so-called "educational" cartoons that show the protagonist overcoming all odds to win in the end of every single episode. Every. Single. Episode. Never losing. Ever! From gold star stickers on pre-school tests to "26.2" stickers on car bumpers, our society teaches us to love winning, instead of teaching us to love. Period. Regardless of winning or losing.

It's OK to feel happiness when we win, to celebrate victory. But it is dangerous to *depend* on winning for happiness. Winning becomes just another drug, like any addictive substance, that hollows us out over time. When we win, we feel good. When we don't, we feel empty. We externalize our self-worth until nothing is left inside.

We need to learn to love without winning. In fact, we need to learn how to love losing. Only then will we learn to truly love. Ourselves, each other, our world. And we can become truly happy. If we don't, we will lose that true love, and we will never be truly happy.

It's our choice: love losing or lose loving.

-7-

LET YOURSELF SUCCEED

On a sunny day in Monterey, California, I walked into my college research mentor's office to ask for a letter of recommendation for my medical school applications. I had spent several months working full time in his laboratory at the Hopkins Marine Station of Stanford University, designing and performing experiments, and I felt he had gotten to know me rather well. My research was progressing very well, and he was always quite complimentary of my work, so I was confident that he would be able to write a strong letter in support of my application. Naturally he agreed to write the letter, but he first asked me for my GPA.

"3.4", I proudly responded.

"That's it?" he replied.

My heart sank. What the hell did he mean, "That's it?"! That was no ordinary 3.4 GPA. That was a *Stanford* 3.4 GPA! Grades at Stanford were based on a curve, and I was surrounded on that curve by some of the smartest young minds in the world. My classmates, with whom I was competing for A's and B's on tests, were geniuses. To hold my own at a 3.4 GPA was one hell of an accomplishment for a small-town boy from Alaska. I was damn proud of that GPA! I was proud to be just hanging with the crowd at such a tough school. Why did my professor have to cut me down?

All of those thoughts went through my head in the split second between him saying "That's it?" and following it immediately with:

"I know you. You're smarter than that."

My sinking heart stopped in its tracks. What did he say? It took me a few more seconds to let that sink in. Was that a compliment? Yes, I think it was. Was he disappointed in my GPA? Yes, he was. But only because he truly believed I could do better.

He didn't know anything about my prior coursework before I joined his lab for a full time research course in marine biology. All he knew was how I thought about problems, proposed and tested hypotheses, and interpreted results. He saw my mind working. He saw me working. He didn't see numbers, grades, or test scores. He formed an unbiased impression of my capabilities. So when he heard my GPA, it didn't fit. Perhaps if he had known my GPA before working with me, he would not have had the same impression of my work. But fortunately, he saw me in action before he knew my GPA. So he knew what I was capable of achieving, even if I hadn't achieved it. Could he be right? Could I be capable of a better GPA than 3.4? At Stanford? And if so, why hadn't I already gotten there?

It wasn't long before I saw the truth. His seemingly harsh comment tore down the veil I had neatly hung around myself when I arrived at Stanford.

I grew up in a small town in Alaska, graduating from a high school where a large number of students dropped out, and only about 20% of those who graduated went on to college. I was the valedictorian, I thought, simply because I did all my homework and studied for my tests. Not because I was particularly smart. I had some athletic accomplishments too, in a sport that was valued at Stanford. And I checked the Alaska box on their class roster, allowing them to say they had students from all fifty states. That's really why I got in. There were Olympic gold medalists and successful entrepreneurs in my college freshman class.

There were inventors and recording artists. There were true geniuses. I was surrounded by people who deserved to be there on their own merits, not because they were from one of the least populated states in the country. I convinced myself that I didn't really belong there. I convinced myself that simply surviving was all I could do. I convinced myself that mediocrity was success.

I have a friend who signs his emails with a quote: "Beware the lollipop of mediocrity. Lick it once and you'll suck forever." I had licked the lollipop of mediocrity as I arrived on campus, and I was still sucking it three years later when my professor's harsh comment pulled it out of my mouth. I had convinced myself to be satisfied with mediocrity. You might ask what's wrong with that? Why not be OK with being average? Shouldn't we be content with wherever we are in the pack? Not everyone can be in the lead, at the top, winning. The trouble is how we get to that place in our minds. I arrived at mediocrity not from contentment, but from self-doubt. I had been a big fish in a small pond in high school, and college suddenly threw me into a much bigger pond with what I thought were much bigger fish. I immediately doubted myself. And that self-doubt choked off my energy flow. My self-doubt became a self-fulfilling prophecy. I believed I could be average, so average I became.

Why must we compare ourselves to others in order to sculpt our sense of self-worth? Why did I have to estimate my rank within the class, before school even started? We love ranking systems. We rank ourselves, even when no external ranking system exists. Who can post the most clever homemade Halloween costume on Pinterest? Who can have the most followers on Twitter or YouTube? Who can make their life look the most completely perfect on Facebook? What if you like to play guitar? You wouldn't post a video of yourself playing guitar unless you knew it would be better than anyone else you know, right? If you want to consider yourself a guitarist, you would hang out with non-guitarists. Otherwise, your self-esteem would take a hit. "I guess I'm not a real guitarist – he's a *real* guitarist!" Instead, you surround yourself with people who are not quite as good as you at what you feel is your most important component of self-esteem. Or you make excuses as to why you are not as good as those around you. And none of that lets you be as good as you can be at anything, or even enjoy anything that you like to do. Like singing, which many of us like to do, but will only do while alone in the shower.

We get in our own way. We do not let ourselves succeed because we are too busy trying to prevent unfavorable comparisons to others.

When I met my marine biology mentor, it was in a small class held off campus at the university's marine station a hundred miles away in Monterey Bay. There were only a handful of students, and we were divided among an equal number of labs. I was not competing with anyone. I was simply doing the work. I had no reason to doubt myself because I had no way of ranking myself against my peers. With the self-doubt gone, the energy flow opened, and great work poured forth. Great work that my mentor saw and appreciated. Great work that made him surprised to hear my GPA from prior courses.

That course did not last forever – I had to go back to the main campus to finish my final year of pre-medical courses. I had to jump back into the big pond.

But I did so with renewed confidence, with a wide open flow of energy, and my GPA rose to a perfect 4.0 for the remainder of my time at Stanford.

That struggle has come up from time to time since college, as I find myself competing where I don't need to compete. And that's when I feel the energy being choked. We must always remember this trap, so that when we feel self-doubt and fear choking our energy, we can step back, get out of our own way, and let ourselves succeed.

-8-

I Am Not the Messiah!

I was told a few years ago by a trusted mentor never to say anything smart in a meeting. If you do, you will undoubtedly get volunteered to chair a subcommittee to address the issue, and suddenly you will have more work to do than you want. Unfortunately, I heard that advice too late in my career. I have a busy surgical practice, and I run a research laboratory. Balancing those two tasks is hard enough. Even harder still is trying to add administrative work. But I went to a meeting once, said something smart, got assigned to a task, performed it well, and next thing you know the senior administrators of the hospital knew me by my first name.

I was asked by one such senior administrator last year to participate on a committee to decrease a particular type of injury risk among employees at our hospital. He was a friend of mine who knew my other commitments, and when he asked me to take on this role, he assured me that I would not be the leader of the committee and that it would involve a minimal time commitment. He had found easy prey. I was addicted to work. Even worse, I was addicted to flattery. All he had to say was something like, "you'd be really good at it," and I was all his. Flattery is addictive, like a drug. I liked praise. I'd seek out praise. I'd follow flattery quite far out of my way, and even into harm's way.

Needless to say, I agreed to join the committee, despite not knowing anything about occupational safety, and despite already having too much on my plate. I arrived at the first meeting, and within about 20 minutes, it became clear to me that everyone else on the committee thought I was the team leader. There were occupational safety experts, administrators, even an Assistant Vice President at the table. But they looked to me as their leader. Becoming increasingly uneasy, I stopped the meeting at one point to clarify roles on the team. I told them flat out that I was not the leader. There was some grumbling, some eyebrow raising, some confusion. But then they all agreed that I was the "physician champion" of the work. Thinking that "champion" meant cheerleader, someone who raises enthusiasm from a position on the sidelines, I agreed to stay on. About six months later, however, I realized that "champion" to everyone else meant team captain. And our team was losing badly because I was sitting on the sidelines. I was the captain of too many other teams to give what I needed to this team. I had known that from the beginning. I knew that all along. But I had been unable to get out of the position of physician champion. Why? I was simply unable to utter the words:

"I am not the Messiah!"

I had heard that the hospital's Chief Operating Officer referred to me as "the Messiah" for my work on the occupational safety team, and I believed it. I fell for it. Who wouldn't fall for such a strong compliment? Yet I became immensely unhappy. I dreaded doing the work, but I dreaded even more *not* doing the work. I was trapped! But why?

I had learned early in my competitive academic life that saying "no" was not allowed. One must seize every opportunity to contribute in order to increase visibility, earn recognition, get promoted, etc. While that strategy may be effective when few opportunities arise, it carries a risk of succeeding too effectively when opportunities begin to multiply. You can very quickly end up doing too much to do any of it well – getting spread too thin. That problem causes stress, affects work performance, relationships, etc. But it cuts even deeper into your own happiness than you allow yourself to admit. But we don't admit it, since multitasking and over-commitment are applauded in our society as signs of productivity and ambition. We let ourselves become trapped in a never-ending cycle of "no good deed goes unpunished".

But there is a way out. Consider the following questions: How can you choose which opportunities to follow? How can you say no to the other opportunities? You already know the answers to those questions. You already have the one skill required to selectively choose opportunities, and the one skill required to reject those that you do not want. In fact, you were born with those skills. Using those skills opens the door to true happiness. You just never use them because they were beaten out of you. What skills are they?

Authenticity and vulnerability.

We all know what we like and what we don't like. But we all too often frame our own preferences in the eyes of society, our peers, the media. What is popular to like? What if you like something quite the opposite? One of my 9-year-old sons loves to dance. He almost never walks in the house – it's always some form of movement closer to dancing. And he has amazing flexibility and strength. He would be a fantastic dancer. Moreover, he despises organized sports such as soccer, basketball, and baseball, so he could devote his free time to dance. So which athletic endeavors has he chosen? Soccer, basketball, and baseball, of course. Why? It's not cool for a boy to dance. His peers have beaten his love for movement out of him, pulling him way off his path of authenticity into a painful place of awkward half-conformity. He becomes the least happy member of each of those teams. As a result, he does not excel at the sports he does not truly enjoy. And that drives him further down. Yet he is tall, muscular, and scary fast, so everyone praises his potential as an athlete. Can you see the trap?

We follow the same external pressures, be they positive, like praise, or negative, like ridicule, more faithfully than we follow our internal desires. We sacrifice authenticity for conformity. We think we can accept ourselves if we are accepted by others. Following this path leads us further and further away from happiness, because it leads us further and further away from our authentic self. We can snap back to happiness if we recognize and value our authentic self as just that: our authentic self. Neither good nor bad, neither right nor wrong, just true. Not dependent on others' impressions or societal "norms".

But how do we get there from here? We have gone so far down the path of what everyone else wants us to do, who everyone else wants us to be, that we feel we cannot get out. We can't find a way, an excuse, to get off the team. But we can. We just need to allow ourselves to use that second skill: vulnerability.

I scheduled a meeting with the hospital COO, the one who called me the Messiah. I didn't tell him the purpose of the meeting, although he knew the topic was employee safety. When the meeting came, I let him talk first. He launched into a monologue of praise and support for my work. He described visions of a brave new world of employee safety thanks to my efforts. He promised great things for my career. A bright future. After about 15 minutes of this, he paused, smiling, fully expecting a chorus of gratitude and cheer, an "Amen" of sorts. That's not what he got. What he got was: "I am not the Messiah."

I tried to let him down gently. I had heard that he liked wine, so I likened myself to a 2005 Bordeaux – a great wine not ready for drinking yet in 2014. I wanted to assure him that I was as good as he thought, but that I wasn't ready to do what he wanted me to do. Yet. I didn't realize at the time that I was still lying. I really didn't want to be as good at administrative work as he thought I could be. I simply didn't like it. I *never* wanted to do that work. It wasn't an issue of "not yet." It was an issue of "not me". Of course, he immediately recognized my ruse. He knew that I was trying to get off the team without admitting that I wasn't the right man for the job, and he called me out. But it was how he responded that shocked me and has since played an important role in my journey to happiness:

"I'm proud of you. Many people can try to make themselves look good by tackling this kind of work. Very few can show the vulnerability that it takes to say they can't do it as well as it needs to be done. Those are the true leaders."

I'm sure I paraphrased what he actually said – I don't remember his exact words because I was so stunned by his acceptance, even praise, of my retreat. Because it wasn't a retreat. It had taken me great courage to schedule a meeting to admit defeat, but he didn't see it as defeat – he saw it as a great triumph of self-awareness. I then recognized why I had looked up to him in particular as a leader over the time I had seen him in his role – vulnerability. He was honest. He was able to connect with everyone else in the hospital, regardless of their role, because he was unafraid to be human. He was vulnerable. He openly admitted that he wasn't perfect.

Nobody's perfect. I'm not perfect. You're not perfect. And the more you try to convince people that you *are* perfect, the more you *actually* convince them that you're not. My wife had been telling me that for years, but it wasn't until I had to admit to the COO that I wasn't the Messiah that I fully understood what she was trying to tell me.

Sure, self-confidence is important. But it doesn't come from pretending to be someone or something that you're not so that other people will respect or accept you. Self-confidence comes from being comfortable with who you are already. You cannot be authentic with others until you are authentic with yourself. You cannot be vulnerable with others unless you are vulnerable with yourself. And you cannot be truly happy unless you allow yourself to be both authentic and vulnerable. But as soon as you allow yourself to use those skills you have had since birth, you will feel the weight of the world lifted from your shoulders. You will breathe a sigh of relief as soon as you realize that nobody truly expects you to be the Messiah. So you shouldn't either.

And then the strangest thing happens. Your newfound freedom allows you to suddenly do a better job of everything, and to continue to get even better at it! You will love what you authentically want to do, and you will be vulnerable enough to see shortcomings as opportunities for improvement. You will excel because you have found happiness, instead of trying to excel in order to find happiness. Just don't let your newfound excellence trick yourself or others into thinking that you're some sort of Messiah!

REACHING ENLIGHTENMENT

-9-

THE EXPERIMENT ALWAYS WORKS

I spend nearly half my professional time in the research laboratory. I am driven by a clinical problem in my specialty that has no known cure – only crude palliative surgeries that only partially address the problem. I am searching for the cure. I know that such a cure is many years away, and finding it will require a deeper understanding of the biology of the problem. Achieving that understanding requires experiments that are difficult to perform and even more difficult to interpret. For in any productive research endeavor, each answer brings more questions. Such is the nature of discovery.

To complicate matters, however, my primary training is as a surgeon. Not a molecular biologist. I have had to learn new tools, techniques, even ways of thinking. It has taken me several years to learn the language alone. Despite this effort, though, I still feel like an outsider in the scientific world. At the worst of times, I have felt like an imposter. At the best of times, I have felt like I might be able to contribute something, but only from my unique position as a surgeon-scientist, not because I am a particularly capable scientist. Either way, I have always felt one step removed from the core culture of science. On the outside looking in. However, after several years of trying to get in, I have recently come to realize that this predicament has given me one of the greatest gifts in my life – not professionally, but on the journey to happiness, even enlightenment.

We all have that friend, you know, the one with the really obvious problem. Maybe they drink too much, maybe they are intolerably arrogant because of obvious insecurity, maybe they pretend to be perfect despite being a hot mess. You can see it. Everyone can see it. Just not them. They are oblivious. Why can't they see it? Because they have assigned a value judgment (good, bad, right, wrong) to their lives, including their issues, so they cannot see the issues for what they really are. They have incorporated their issues into their self-image, their self-worth, their very identity. They cannot tackle them objectively because they cannot see them objectively. But they would be so easy to address if they could just open their eyes!

Guess what? You too have problems that you cannot see objectively, but others can see easily. For every intervention you want to stage for your friends, your friends want to stage an intervention for you. What if you could learn to see your own issues as clearly as others do? You can. If there has been one important discovery in my laboratory research to date, it is how to do just that. Really, you ask? In a molecular biology laboratory?

The scientific method is really pretty simple. If you have a question, and no one knows the answer, you guess. That guess, based on available knowledge, is called an hypothesis. You then test that hypothesis by doing an experiment. You have an expectation about how the experiment will end up – you expect it to support your hypothesis. Or maybe it will refute your hypothesis, rule it out. Either way, you will learn valuable information. The trouble is that we get too attached to our hypotheses to see the results of the experiments objectively. The essence of that problem can be summed up in four words uttered by a young scientist who was dead set on proving a particular hypothesis:

"The experiment didn't work."

He had designed an elaborate, but methodologically sound, experiment to test his revolutionary hypothesis, and when that experiment failed to support his hypothesis, he immediately discarded it as invalid. It hadn't worked. It hadn't proven his hypothesis. And in so doing, it hadn't proven him right. It hadn't validated his claim to scientific fame. It hadn't sped him on his course to career advancement. Like a mad scientist whose plan for world domination was just thwarted, he actually progressed through all of the emotional states of grief right before my eyes!

I was dumbfounded. Not because he was reacting so strongly to his experimental result, but because he was missing the fact that his experiment had actually revealed an important piece of information that could change the course of his research in a new and exciting way. The experiment *had* worked! It answered a question. The experiment stood at a fork in the road, and it very clearly pointed out which road to take, which direction to follow. The trouble is that the scientist who performed the experiment had allowed himself to assign value to the other direction before the experiment was even performed. He had judged his hypothesis as correct, simply because it was his idea, his guess. If he had not made that judgment, assigned that value, he would have seen as clearly as I did that the experiment *had* worked.

In fact, the experiment *always* works.

What if, for the sake of argument, the experiment neither supports nor refutes a given hypothesis? It fails to point in one direction or other at the fork in the road. Maybe the chemicals weren't mixed properly. Maybe the technique wasn't performed properly. Maybe the experimental design wasn't methodologically sound. Aren't those all legitimate reasons that experiment might "not work"? But even those failures teach you something. A "failed" experiment can teach you that that certain combination of chemicals, techniques, experimental designs, etc. will not answer your question. You still learn how to improve your methods. You always learn from an experiment, even if it's not to do it that way again. You always learn. And what is the point of experimentation if not to learn? The experiment always works!

So why didn't this scientist understand that the experiment had worked? Because he had his heart set on a particular outcome. He had allowed himself to *want* a certain result. He was emotionally invested. He valued an anticipated outcome, so he judged the actual outcome as *bad*. If he hadn't assigned value to that result, he wouldn't have judged the outcome of the experiment as good or bad, failure or success. He would have been able to take the information and move to the next step. It was easy for me to avoid assigning value to the experimental outcome, because I wasn't the one doing that actual research. I was on the outside looking in. But it was very hard for the scientist doing the work. Why? Because he was emotionally invested in the work. His career depends on scientific successes. He needs to demonstrate a track record of experiments that prove him right, and then propose experiments he is sure will continue to prove him right. He is trapped. But that model of success actually stifles innovation, chokes off the flow of creative energy. We cling too long to bad ideas and miss opportunities to seize good ideas that stare us in the face, all because we allow ourselves to become attached to ideas through value judgments. Conversely, some of the greatest advancements in science have arisen from serendipitous, unexpected outcomes, not hoped-for results from predictable experiments. We just need to let go of judgments in order to capture those opportunities.

So what does all of this have to do with happiness? Our life is nothing more than a series of experiments. We can form expectations, hope for certain outcomes, assign value to external events, or even our internal thoughts and feelings, and judge the world and ourselves according to those values. Or we can simply accept what is as exactly that: what is.

My favorite analogy describes life's events, as well as our thoughts and feelings, as cars on a highway. We can sit safely on the side of the highway watching those cars go by. There are big ugly ones that we don't like, there are cool fast ones that we do like, and there are millions that we don't even notice go by. We are totally fine watching the traffic until we run out into the road. Why would we run into the road? At times, we run out into the road to chase after the cars we like. For example, we try to hold onto the feeling we get from hearing praise – so we chase after it as it starts to fade. But that initial feeling is fleeting, and we will never be able to hold onto it forever. But if we try to catch it and keep it, like chasing a car passing on the highway, we end up out there on the highway in the middle of the traffic. We're going to get run over. At other times, we run out to try to stop the big ugly ones – like the sadness from being rejected or from losing a loved one. Try as we might to hold it at bay, we cannot stop it from entering our mind, from entering our field of view on the highway. If we try to stop it, we are out there on the highway again and we will get run over. Either way, even if we manage to not get run over, we block the traffic and disrupt the flow of thoughts, emotions, energy, and life itself through our minds.

We must sit on the side of the highway. On the outside looking in, from a position of clarity.

Sound impossible? It's not. As a surgeon, I can sit by the side of the science highway, watching experiments go by. I can see them for what they are and let myself learn objectively from them. I am not emotionally invested in any particular outcomes, for every outcome has meaning. And if I can sit and watch that part of my life from my seat of safety and clarity on the side of the highway, then I can do the same for the rest of my life. I can witness experiences, emotions, thoughts, desires, regrets, hopes, and fears enter my mind, and I can let them go by. I don't try to catch the "good" ones or stop the "bad" ones. I can let go of judgement, and once I have, I can watch the events of life unfold and accept them for what they are. For once the event has unfolded, there is nothing else it can be. It is what it is. It does no good to assign it judgment as good or bad.

This approach takes practice. We have to become aware of the temptations to pass judgment, to run out into the road. But with enough practice, our default tendency will be to sit calmly on the side of the road. Peace will abound. Happiness will become the default. That place is enlightenment.

-10-

THE FREEDOM OF CAPTIVITY

One day after school when I was nine years old, my father drove my brother and me to a large building with bizarre equipment in it and left us there with a gruff man with an impossibly bushy mustache. It was a gymnastics gym, and that man was a gymnastics coach. We had no idea what to do there, or even why we were there. Over the next hour, we learned exercises, strange body positions, rules, and even what seemed to be a whole new language. Yet we loved it. And we were very tired when we got back in the car to go home. Upon arriving back at home, our mother told us that we had been put in a gymnastics class because we were too wild at home. We had too much energy, and it needed to be put to good use. Channeled. Focused. Was it a punishment? Or a reward? Hard to tell, but it had worked – we were spent!

That day has turned out to be one of the most important gifts my parents have ever given me.

At first, it seemed like we were being shooed out of the house to "get our crazies out". They just didn't want us wrestling at home and breaking any more furniture. But over time, the role of gymnastics in my life changed dramatically. My brother eventually became more interested in rodeo horse racing, but I stuck with gymnastics. I competed through high school, even traveling to the Olympic Training Center twice on the road toward the 1992 Olympics. That level of commitment took work. Throughout adolescence, I was in the gym for hours at a time, at least 5 days a week. And that commitment took a toll, especially socially. I was clueless about the dating scene in high school since I spent every evening in the gym. I was perfectly happy wearing lycra in front of a bunch of girls in the gym, but a bumbling idiot trying to ask a girl out on a date at school. Needless to say, I heard "no" a lot from the girls at school. Adolescence for me was especially awkward. But there was one place where none of that mattered. There was a safe place, a place where I was completely free.

That safe place was a place of grave danger. That freedom arose from the most rigid captivity.

Nine feet off the ground, upside down, and flying around a stainless steel bar holding on with only one hand. At the top of a one-handed 'giant' swing on the horizontal bar. No room for error, at risk of serious injury, completely locked into the task at hand, I was truly captivated. At that moment, and any similar moments in the sport, there are no crushes, girlfriends, rejections, bad days, good days. There are no fights with your brother. There are no upset parents. There are no difficult homework assignments. There is nothing. Nothing but pure presence. The rest of the world melts away, displaced by the need to focus on the present. You can't give any attention to the past or the future – not even the next move on the bar. All your mental energy is devoted to just that one moment. And each moment was like that. Gymnastics forced me to be present, and in so doing, taught me the joy of being present. For in being present is happiness.

Have you ever been captivated by a task? Have you ever been so into a moment that you forgot all your worries? Even if it is for a fleeting second, it is a wonderful holiday from the distractions, fears and regrets we tend to carry with us. What if we could live in that holiday all the time? We've all been to vacation spots where we fantasize about buying a house – we could live there all the time – wouldn't that be wonderful? But no, we need to go back to work, back to reality. But what if we could live in a vacation destination AND work in the real world at the same time?

I am no longer a gymnast. A broken neck ended my career before I was able to make it to the Olympics. But I have been able to find a similar joy of being present in my work. I am very lucky to have the privilege to perform surgery. During the time that I am operating on a patient, I am completely locked into the task at hand. This time, the risk is not to my neck, but to the child under my care. Many surgeons feel this same way. There are pagers, cell phones, nurses to ask questions, other patients on the schedule for the day, stresses of home life and academic pursuits, and yes, good days and bad days. But none of those thoughts distract the mind that is fully present in the task at hand. Surgery is a time when the mind is not allowed to wander, and thus it is a time when the mind is completely free to be present.

But why do we have to be "free to be present"? Why do we need permission, or to be forced to be present? We as a society are always trying to stay one step ahead – in the future. We have to be thinking about the next move before we are finished with the current task. We are always after the next big thing. The latest, greatest technology. We wait in lines overnight to be the first to get the newest phone, even though we have a perfectly good one in our pocket (that we waited in line for overnight a year ago). Today itself is already obsolete. And it's not just linear, it's spatial too – we have to be everywhere at all times. We praise the multitasker. We sit at dinner with our friends, all staring at our individual phone screens, interacting with other friends on social networking sites, reading news articles or gossip, or posting pictures of what we are eating so the world can share it with us. And in the process, we lose touch with the present.

Here's a disheartening example. The Pope came to visit the United States last month. Very important people undoubtedly paid very large sums of money to be standing in certain spots where they would have a chance to come face to face with the Pope. Did they? No.

They came face to *phone* to face with the Pope. A cell phone was in front of nearly every face to document the moment. The people holding those phones and staring at those screens did not even see the pope with their naked eye at the very moment they cherished enough to document so carefully. Why? Because we place value on *having had* the experience, not on actually *having* the experience. We actually give up the present in order to document the past for the future.

These societal pressures make it nearly impossible to justify simply being present. We never give ourselves permission to be present, even though we have all experienced, even for a fleeting moment, the joy of that state. So we only feel that freedom when we are forced to be present. On the high bar, in the operating room. But we can choose to do it. And it works just as well, or even better.

I ran my first ultramarathon three days ago. With only five miles to go, I realized that there was no way that I was going to finish under my goal time. I was not dejected, though. I did not give up. I simply tried dropping my focus on the clock five miles away. And I did so by choosing to be present. In the forest, on the trail, surrounded by beautiful fall foliage, aware of the gift of my sore legs still running after all those miles, aware of the blister on my heel that signified the effort I had put in. I simply chose to be present. And a veil lifted. I could see the world, the experience more clearly. My legs became lighter, the ground softer. I passed a couple of runners on the trail who looked like they needed help. I stopped to offer them nutrition and water that I had with me. I subconsciously gave myself permission to notice the pain in their strides and to slow down to help them despite what it would do to my finishing time. It was a part of being present rather than worrying about how far in the future I would cross the finish line. Being present allowed connectedness.

And at some point in the last mile, rather than reaching the anticipated cathartic awareness that I was about to finish an ultramarathon, I came to the cathartic awareness that I was indeed fully present, and that all my concerns, my fears, my pain – physical and emotional - had melted away. I felt the same freedom that I had felt while captivated by the high bar in gymnastics, or in a complex surgery in the operating room. Only it was in my power now: that freedom of captivity. I could control it. I realized I could give myself the gift of being present. Anywhere, anytime, all the time. I had reached true happiness, not happiness that depended upon finishing an ultramarathon under my goal finishing time, but just pure happiness. I had reached enlightenment in that moment in the woods.

Three minutes later, I crossed the finish line. One minute under my goal finishing time. As if with a wink and a nod, fate was telling me I had indeed reached my goal.

So whatever your goal, know that you are already there. You just have to let yourself *be present* there. Anywhere, everywhere. The door is not locked. Step back, let it open, and you are there.

-11-

SITTING AT THE LOOM OF LIFE

I remember learning as a very young child the smell of wool. My brother and I would help shear the sheep at the state fair. We would wash the wool and run it through the hand-powered carding drum to separate the fibers from the debris caught in the wool. Then the piles of wool were ready for the next spinning bee, where my mother and her friends would get together to spin the wool into yarn on foot-powered, wooden spinning wheels. The spinning bees would take place in our living room, overlooking aspen trees on the Alaskan hillside outside the long wall of tall windows at the front of our log home. It was always a very peaceful scene.

Once spun, most of the yarn would be knitted into hats and sweaters. But some of the yarn made it onto the loom for weaving. My mother's first loom was small enough to sit on a table, and the weaving started out fairly basic. Wall-hangings, scarves, table runners. But the looms and weaving got more and more elaborate as my mother grew in her craft. Eventually, my brother and I helped my father construct a loom that occupied an entire bedroom. On that loom, the most intricate designs would unfold in tapestries, line by line, over months and months. Whenever my mother would have time, she would sit at that loom, adding a few more inches to the tapestry. We would watch it come to life, little by little, until a complete picture was formed.

And what a beautiful picture it always was when it was done!

What amazed me most, however, was not the beauty of the finished product, but that the artistry was accomplished by no more than a single strand of yarn being woven through a second, seemingly random, array of parallel yarns. The longitudinal strands, termed the "warp", are set on the loom first, and appear only as collection of parallel lines with no image, no meaning. But when the other yarn, termed the "weft", is woven horizontally through the warp, the image appears.

And that weft is only a single strand of yarn. One strand, woven skillfully through an otherwise uninterpretable warp. The images created in weaving are simply the result of how the warp and weft are woven together. You don't need fancy yarns. You can create a beautiful tapestry simply by mastering the weaving.

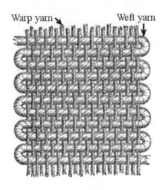

Only at the end of this book do I now realize that such is life as well. A single strand of yarn woven through randomness to create meaning. Your world is the warp, a complex array of parallel threads: your work, your home, your relationships, your hobbies. All the demands on your time. All the events in your world. Just like one cannot change the warp on a loom once it is set, one cannot change the world of what is. What we *can* control is the weft, and how it is woven through the warp. And that weft is your mind, that single, unbroken strand of yarn, woven through your world to create the tapestry that is your life. We can master how we let our mind interact with the world. We can master the art of weaving at the loom of life.

We can walk through the unlocked door of happiness without having to change the world around us if we recognize the power of stepping back into our mind.

We can see beauty in the world, even when we are very down, if we allow ourselves to ask what else is possible.

We can open up the possibility of truly enjoying the world by simply deciding to truly enjoy it.

We can be grateful for all of the wonderful, albeit simple, blessings in this world if we stop focusing on what we want - what we don't have.

We can love ourselves unconditionally, even when we "lose", if we learn to love losing for what it can teach us.

We can let go of feelings of sadness, hurt, loneliness, loss, or any other pain that arises if we understand that we cannot *be* those feelings.

We can get out of our own way, let our energy flow, and let ourselves succeed in the world if we value ourselves without needing to compare ourselves to others.

We can happily and peacefully excel in what we truly value if we allow ourselves to be authentic and vulnerable.

We can learn and grow in response to whatever the world throws at us if we learn to take a step back from our emotional reactivity.

And we can find unbridled peace, happiness and enlightenment by simply choosing to be present in the world. Anytime. Anywhere.

And this point is the most important. We don't have to disappear from the world as we know it to find enlightenment. We don't have to give up our worldly aspirations to find happiness. We can choose happiness and find enlightenment right now. Right here. Right in the middle of our crazy, hectic world. And that enlightenment can have immediate positive effects on our life as we know it. If you don't believe me, remember that my moment of enlightenment during my recent ultramarathon, permitted by giving up on my finishing time and choosing simply to be present, got me to the finish line under my goal time and against all odds, even though I stopped twice to help others. Giving up on running fast - instead, just enjoying the running - made me run faster!

So we needn't choose between our real-world life and happiness. It is not one or the other. It is one *and* the other. It is the world and the mind woven together into a tapestry of happiness. We are each sitting at our loom of life, and our tapestry tells the story of our journey. We can look back at where we've been, without the ability or need to change what's already woven. But we can determine where our journey goes by weaving our tapestry mindfully moving forward. The tapestry on my loom is looking better. Line by line. Little by little. And I'm still weaving. Your tapestry can be beautiful too. You just need to take that first step. That first step through the door of happiness.

And that door, my friend, is not locked.

THANK YOU

Nothing of what you have read here is new. I have lived all of the stories of my life I have told, but the thoughts, realizations, conclusions, and advice arising from those stories have all existed for centuries. They have simply been awoken within me by many great teachers. My wife, my children, my parents and brother. My mentors: Mara Kleinman, Scott Steel, and Jill Weaver, especially. My good friend, Steve Luckenbach. And all of the players in the stories. There are also many great books and resources on mindfulness and enlightenment, but those that have been the most influential in my recent journey are *Happiness Is a Choice* by Barry Kaufman, *The Untethered Soul* by Michael Singer, and Headspace.com.

But most importantly, I thank you, the reader, the fellow soul on the journey of life, the journey toward happiness, for sharing with me the belief that true happiness is an achievable goal. Thank you for walking through the unlocked door with me. It makes my own journey easier to know that you are right there with me.

Image Credits

Cover: "Door to Freedom" modified with license from http://www.canstockphoto.com/door-to-freedom-0390767.html. 3D rendering by Spectral.

Chapter 1: Modified from "Aufseß Bier" by User Benreis at https://commons.wikimedia.org/wiki/File:Aufse%C3%9F_Bier.JPG#/media/File:Aufse%C3%9F_Bier.JPG

Chapter 2: Bright orange (really) car. By User Aero777 at https://commons.wikimedia.org/wiki/File:2013_Subaru_XV_2.0 i_in_Cyberjaya,_Malaysia_(02).jpg

Chapter 3: In public domain at https://commons.wikimedia.org/wiki/File:Young_woman_under_the_shower.jpg

Chapter 4: Marnie, Roger, and Peter Cornwall in Fairbanks, Alaska, September 2015. Photo by Roger Cornwall.

Chapter 5: Andouillette sausage. By User DocteurCosmos at https://commons.wikimedia.org/wiki/File:Andouillette_%22%C3%A0_la_ficelle%22_cuite_au_barbecue.jpg

Chapter 6: Clouds receding over the Gulkana Glacier in the Alaska Range. Photo by Roger Cornwall.

Chapter 7: Hopkins Marine Station of Stanford University. Image in public domain at https://commons.wikimedia.org/wiki/File:Agassiz_Building,_Hopkins_Marine_Station.JPG

Chapter 8: John the Baptist recognizes Jesus as the messiah. Stipple engraving by F. Bartolozzi, 1765, after Domenichino. Wellcome Trust. Iconographic Collections.https://commons.wikimedia.org/wiki/File:John_the_Baptist_recognises_Jesus_as_the_messiah._Stipple_en_Wellcome_V0034696.jpg

Chapter 9: Mad Scientist. By User JJ at https://commons.wikimedia.org/wiki/File:Mad_scientist_bw.svg

Chapter 10: Gymnast's hands on the horizontal bar. By User Raphael Goetter at https://commons.wikimedia.org/wiki/File:Horizontal_bar_(hands).jpg

Chapter 11: Warp and weft in weaving. By User Ryj at https://en.wikipedia.org/wiki/File:Warp_and_weft.jpg

Made in the USA
Monee, IL
13 January 2022